A graceful 1939 SS Jaguar drophead coupé with wartime headlamp blinds and contemporary windscreen demister.

THE JAGUAR

Andrew Whyte
(Third edition revised by Jonathan Wood)

Shire Publications

CONTENTS

Published in 2007 by Shire Publications Ltd, Cromwell House, Church Street, Princes Risborough, Buckinghamshire HP27 9AA, UK. Copyright © 1987 by the estate of Andrew Whyte and 2007 by Jonathan Wood. First edition 1987; reprinted 1990. Second edition 1999. Third edition 2007. Shire Album 196. ISBN 978 0 7478 0663 9.

Printed in Great Britain by Ashford Colour Press Ltd, Unit 600, Fareham Reach, Fareham Road, Gosport, Hants PO13 0FW.

British Library Cataloguing in Publication Data: Whyte, Andrew (Andrew John Appleton) The Jaguar. – 3rd ed. – (Shire album; 196) 1. Jaguar automobile 2. Jaguar automobile – History I. Title II. Wood, Jonathan 629.2'222 ISBN-13: 978 0 7478 0663 9.

Editorial Consultant: Michael E. Ware, former Director of the National Motor Museum, Beaulieu.

ACKNOWLEDGEMENTS
All illustrations are from the author's collection or by courtesy of Jaguar Archive. This third edition has been revised by Jonathan Wood.

COVER: *Jaguar's acclaimed XK, launched in 2006, received the coveted Car of the Year award and plaudits from the press and public alike. (Jaguar Cars)*

BACK COVER: *A 1987 model Jaguar XJ6 ('Sovereign' variant) and a 1951 Jaguar Mark Seven, photographed by the author at Glamis Castle, Scotland. (Cars by courtesy of Jaguar Cars Ltd and Mr Peter Cooper respectively.)*

LEFT: *William Lyons riding his Harley-Davidson at Blackpool, about 1920.*

Austin Swallow production gets under way in spacious new premises at Coventry in 1929. Note the neat hardtop (left foreground). The 'railway line' is a relic of the factory's use for shell filling in the First World War.

THE SWALLOW SIDECAR
AND COACHBUILDING COMPANY

In September 1935 the name 'Jaguar' was chosen for a new range of cars by 34-year-old William Lyons, who was making a fresh start in his business. Since his 21st birthday Lyons had been held back by his partner, William Walmsley, who did not share his driving ambition, but at the end of 1934 Walmsley had departed, preferring early retirement and his model railway to sharing the running of a rapidly growing motor-car manufacturing company. Thus Lyons was sole proprietor of the newly formed SS Cars Limited, later to be renamed Jaguar Cars Limited.

Lyons's special skills were in the fields of commerce and marketing. In his youth he had transferred from an apprenticeship with the reputable vehicle builders Crossley of Manchester to car salesmanship in his home town of Blackpool.

In his spare time he rode motorcycles competitively and socially, and he soon bought a 'Zeppelin'-shaped sidecar from a neighbour, Walmsley. Walmsley's sidecars — first built in Stockport in 1920, then, from 1921, in Blackpool — were called Swallow. Their quality and spectacular looks appealed to Lyons, and he recommended ways of making more of them, and more cheaply, to meet the evident demand for economical personal transport.

The men became partners and, with £500 backing from each of their fathers, they formed the Swallow Sidecar Company in 1922. Within five years they had moved into bigger premises and, now with a small staff, branched out into the manufacture of shapely special bodies for the everyday type of car chassis that was normally fitted with a simple, box-like

3

structure to shelter its driver and passengers. The Swallow-bodied Austin Seven open two-seater introduced in 1927 could best be described as 'cheap and cheerful' and retailed for £175.

The new Henly group requested the alternative of an Austin Seven Swallow saloon. Fortunately Swallow now had a first-class coachmaker, trained at Lanchester's, Cyril Holland, who drew a saloon body on the workshop wall and established the means of making it. A Morris Cowley-Swallow was built, too, but not followed up.

By 1928 the facilities in Blackpool were not adequate to meet Henly's required delivery targets. At Lyons's instigation, Swallow moved from Blackpool to Coventry and occupied one of the disused blocks of a First World War shell-packing factory. It was not salubrious but there was space into which to expand, and the central location was much more convenient for supply and distribution.

The Swallow Sidecar and Coachbuilding Company may have seemed to be just one of many similar small specialised organisations, but when other firms went

Lyons's first overseas agent, Emil Frey of Zürich, with his Swallow sidecar outfit, about 1927.

4

down after the Wall Street Crash of October 1929 Swallow continued to expand. The reasons were the instant visual appeal and the remarkable value of its products.

After the Austin Seven came Fiat, Standard, Swift and Wolseley Swallows. The Wolseleys were open two-seaters and four-seaters on the six-cylinder Hornet chassis; the others were saloons.

The sidecar department carried on throughout the 1930s but it was not expanded much. Lyons saw that his future lay in the motor car. Henlys encouraged Swallow. They were bringing each other more and more business.

An important development came in 1931. In that year the Standard Motor Company was supplying four-cylinder and six-cylinder chassis to Swallow. It

Austin Seven Swallow production two-seater (above) and prototype saloon (below) in 1928.

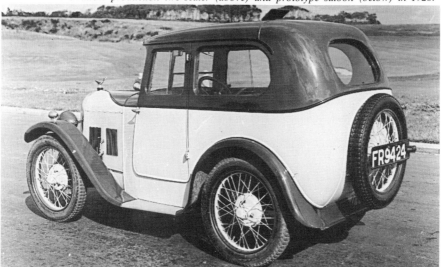

The SWALLOW HAS ARRIVED!

SPORTS BODIES
for the Connoisseur

The perfection of body-building art developed upon new and better lines. Grace, exquisite finish, greater comfort and better protection, feature in all Swallow products.

HENLYS have been appointed Sole Distributors for the Southern Counties (excepting Kent), and are offering these striking bodies on specially tuned Austin 7 and Morris Chassis at the following attractive prices.

A fine selection of beautiful colour schemes is available. The features include cowl over radiator, Vee screen, draught-proof side curtains or coupe head, etc. For early delivery orders should be placed now.

These bodies transform the Austin into a real car— giving big car comfort and lines. The bodies on the Cowley Chassis introduce an entirely new Morris model.

The MORRIS Cowley Model

The AUSTIN 7 Swallow

PRICES:

	Swallow Austin	Swallow Morris
With cape hood only	£175	£220
With coupe saloon head only	£185	£230
With cape hood and interchangeable coupe saloon head	£190	£235

Irrefutably my dear...
THE CAR OF THE YEAR

ABOVE: *The first SS1, introduced at the 1931 London Motor Show. It was a two-seater; the hood irons were for decoration only. Five hundred were made.*
BELOW: *After just one year, the SS1 became a full four-seater fixed-head coupé of considerable beauty. Announced in September 1932, it had an underslung chassis.*

RIGHT: *The last new SS1 to be introduced, in the spring of 1935, was this smart SS1 drophead coupé. Note the armchair-style rear seating.*

SS1 and SS2 production lines, early 1935. The coachbuilder is on the verge of becoming a true motor manufacturer.

was clear to all that Swallow bodies were unusual and potentially attractive, but the designer was frustrated by his inability to put his ideas into effect. Towering radiators and high chassis members were still the norm in Britain, where the average car (for those lucky enough to have one) tended to be a little black box. From the outset the Swallow body had proved that curves and colours did not have to be costly, but the stance was high and the low roof was achieved only by adopting a shallow windscreen. This was particularly noticeable on the Standard Swallow. Lyons overcame the problem by reaching agreement with Standard on the supply of specially lowered chassis, exclusive to Swallow. Thus was the 'SS' marque created, although it was decided by both parties not to treat the letters as

initials for anything in particular.

The six-cylinder SS1 and four-cylinder SS2 gave Lyons the opportunity to style his cars in the unrestricted way he wanted. The SS1 models from 1933 were long and low, yet very well proportioned. The aura inside was chic. The performance, however, was adequate rather than sporting. In this respect, the SS flattered to deceive.

The split between Lyons and Walmsley occurred as Lyons developed plans to become a true motor manufacturer, not merely a coachbuilder and sidecar maker. Once Walmsley had taken his money and left, Lyons could take all the decisions on his own, and his most important step in early 1935 was to set up an engineering department to be run by William Munger Heynes.

8

The original 1936 model SS Jaguar 2.7 litre saloon with coachbuilt body and side-mounted spare wheel, priced at £385. (George Matthews is the driver in this contemporary Welsh Rally scene.)

THE EARLY JAGUARS

William Heynes came to SS from Humber in April 1935, when he was 31 years old; he was to remain in charge of vehicle engineering, up to and including the XJ6, until he retired in 1969. Before Heynes's arrival, the independent consulting engineer Harry Weslake had begun working on an overhead-valve conversion of Standard's side-valve 2.7 litre six-cylinder engine for William Lyons's latest project, the completely new SS Jaguar.

The six-cylinder model was described as 'a credit to the British automobile industry' by *The Autocar*, while *The Motor* of 24th September 1935, the day the SS Jaguar range was announced, stated that 'with a distinguished appearance, outstanding performance and attractive price as the main characteristics, the new SS Jaguar range represents an achievement of which Mr. Lyons and his technical staff may well feel proud'.

The star of the new Jaguars was a sleek four-door saloon — thoroughly original yet hinting more at Bentley than referring back to earlier SSs. The looks and the price of £385 were right, as ever, but it had good performance, too: it could reach 85 mph (137 km/h) and cruise at 70 mph (113 km/h) (where there were roads to do so). At the same time a smaller version of the new saloon appeared, with the SS2's Standard four-cylinder 1.6 litre power unit. This was the only car with a side-valve engine ever to go on the market bearing the Jaguar name.

Two open tourers were also announced, featuring new chassis and the overhead-valve six-cylinder engine. They created less interest than the saloon, however, the bodywork being familiar from the obsolescent SS1 range. One was a four-seater, the other a short-chassis two-seater sports model called the SS Jaguar 100. It retained Lyons's attractive styling but also proved itself technically competent by making the best performance in the 1936 Alpine Trial, the first of several competition successes for the new marque.

The pressed-steel bodied 1938 model SS Jaguar 2.7 and 3.5 litre saloons were re-introduced after the Second World War as plain Jaguars. This is one of them (the pre-war cars had a slightly thicker plated waist-band). The leaping jaguar was an accessory in those days.

Production doubled from little more than 1700 cars in the 1934-5 model year to well over 3500 in the year ending 31st July 1937. Then, because of the switch from the traditional wood-frame body construction of the traditional coachbuilder to the more modern pressed steel method, sales fell to little more than two thousand in 1938, but they soared again next year, reaching five thousand before the outbreak of the Second World War. By that time an additional 3.5 litre version of the existing six-cylinder engine was being offered, and the four-seater tourer had been replaced by a much more weatherproof and luxurious drophead coupé. The 1938 3.5 litre SS Jaguar 100 two-seater was the cheapest 100 mph (160 km/h) car on the British market, at £445. A further attraction to the more conservative buyer was the introduction of an overhead-valve four-cylinder engined saloon for the 1938-9 season.

This boost gave SS Cars Limited sufficient reputation for it to be entrusted with war contracts, although for a while it

Mrs McLennan and her navigator revel in the mud of a late 1930s SS Car Club rally. The SS Jaguar 100 was Britain's first genuine 100 mph (160 km/h) car which could be bought for under £500.

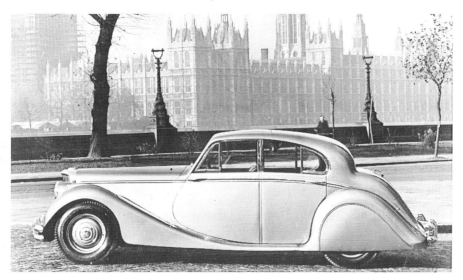

The Jaguar Mark Five (1948–51) as a four-door saloon. This is one of the original publicity shots.

looked as if the work would not be forthcoming. Then came a major order for the traditional Swallow product, the sidecar, and all was well. Aircraft repairs and component manufacture were supplemented by special trailers and other more mundane products. There was opportunity for design work, too, and SS's chief development engineer, Walter Hassan, and their designer, Claude Baily, worked on miniature jeep-type vehicles intended for parachute drops.

The war work helped the company to build up its manufacturing facilities and, while the Swallow sidecar business was sold off, SS Cars Limited came out of the conflict as an established motor manufacturer. When peace was restored, William Lyons changed the company name: 'Jaguar' had become well known on the product badge, so it became the title of the firm, too. He also re-introduced proved pre-war style cars in order to resume production quickly, while new chassis were designed for announcement later on. Some other manufacturers, who tried to bring in new designs almost at once, enjoyed only brief success despite the undoubted quality of their product. For example, two Coventry marques,

Alvis and Lea-Francis, were never able to modernise or to build up production to an economic level.

Wisely, Lyons did not re-introduce the '100' model with his post-war range in August 1945. The two-seater had never sold in great numbers. He knew that volume sales were essential – and, in particular, exports. His pioneering work in popularising the Jaguar car from New York to Hollywood paid off handsomely. He visited New York and California, showing off his wares to the film stars who had previously bought Duesenbergs, Cords or other exotic cars from now defunct American companies. The age of mouth-organ grilles and flying buttresses was about to hit North America and Lyons could see a market for the conservative British style his Jaguars offered. Although he had not intended to do so, because they were time-consuming to build, Lyons re-introduced the 2.7 and 3.5 litre six-cylinder drophead coupés in 1947, especially for export.

Lyons wanted to maintain his company's rate of expansion. Its export performance made it easier to obtain the materials necessary to increase production, for money was scarce in post-war

Britain and anyone who could earn American dollars in quantity deserved all possible encouragement.

From the late 1930s, when the well known racing car engineer Walter Hassan had joined Heynes's team to develop future models, there had been a Citroën-inspired independent torsion-bar front suspension system on the stocks. In 1948 it became the main talking point of a new chassis, the Mark Five, announced in September 1948 in good time for London's first post-war Motor Show. The familiar pushrod overhead-valve (ohv) 2.7 and 3.5 litre six-cylinder engines (for which Lyons had bought the machine tools from Standard) were still used, and the bodywork, though different in most details, was essentially similar in style to that of the original SS Jaguar. A saloon and a drophead coupé were again offered. The latter was the last model of that kind to be included in the Jaguar range.

In the spring of 1949 the last four-cylinder Jaguars were made. Because of their poor power-to-weight ratio and the inadequacy of the engine for the Mark Five chassis Jaguar was suddenly without a 'compact' car range. This gap would be filled in the late 1950s, by which time most post-war restrictions had been lifted and there was, once again, a British public to serve.

The Jaguar XK120 prototype at the 1948 Earls Court show. Only a very few early cars had this straight-sided windscreen.

Ian Appleyard was Britain's best rally driver of the early post-war period. Most of his successes were achieved with these two cars: the SS Jaguar 100 (left) in the 1940s, and its successor, the Jaguar XK120, in the 1950s. (This is a 1970s photograph.)

JAGUAR SPORTS

The 1948 London Motor Show at Earls Court, the first for ten years, was Britain's first opportunity to look forward to the freedom of peacetime motoring despite rationing (and all the other post-war restrictions) and many manufacturers took full advantage of it, notably Jaguar of Coventry. Jaguar's main exhibit was the new Mark Five but this model was overshadowed by a dramatic-looking XK open two-seater. The first catalogue intimated that there would be a choice of 2 litre four-cylinder or 3.4 litre six-cylinder versions of a brand-new double overhead-camshaft (dohc) XK engine.

The Jaguar XK Super Sports, as it was dubbed initially, had been created very quickly and the one on show in 1948 was not drivable, but it drew the crowds and press comment because of its beautiful roadster bodywork. Although preparations to produce the smaller engine were well advanced, it was shelved in 1949 and never revived. On the other hand, the six-cylinder XK engine was to prove one of the most successful high-performance

power units there has ever been, and it was still being produced for special purposes nearly forty years later. William Heynes, Walter Hassan and Claude Baily are credited with its original design.

In 1949 the XK120 was got ready for a limited production run, said to be only two hundred cars. Experience had told William Lyons that production quantities should be kept low, expecially as this was not an economy sports car like the MG.

An XK120 was taken to the Belgian autoroute in the summer of 1949 and test driver R. M. V. Sutton proved it capable of a genuine 120 mph (193 km/h) as its name suggested. Indeed, it exceeded 130 mph (210 km/h), which at that time was prodigious. More important, the car was free of temperament. Later that year XK120s driven by Leslie Johnson and Peter Walker came first and second in the first production car race at Silverstone, instigated by the *Daily Express*, sponsors of the meeting, to promote the post-war revival of Britain's motor industry.

Film stars Michael Wilding and Elizabeth Taylor in a Jaguar XK120 on the set of 'The Girl Who Had Everything' in Hollywood in the early 1950s.

The beautiful Jaguar XK120 fixed-head coupé (1951-4). The wheel spat has already been dented.

From 1954 the XK120 was replaced by the XK140. Again, the options included roadster, fixed-head and (seen here) drophead coupé bodies.

The final series of XK sports and GT cars was the XK150, which was made from mid 1957 to late 1960. The little S on the door of this fixed-head coupé means that it has a triple-carburettor engine.

The XK120's first major win was by Stirling Moss at Dundrod, Northern Ireland, in the 1950 Tourist Trophy race. Between 1950 and 1953 Ian Appleyard's XK120 won the first Alpine Gold Cup ever awarded, two RAC Rallies, the Tulip Rally and many more events. It took drivers of high calibre such as Moss and Appleyard to win major competitions with what was a docile high-performance touring car. Others performed outstandingly with the XK120, however, none more so than Johnny Claes, the only man to win the *Marathon de la Route* (Liège-Rome-Liège) without loss of marks. He did so in 1951. One of the greatest feats of endurance, to average over 100 mph (160 km/h) for a whole week, was achieved by Stirling Moss, Leslie Johnson, Jack Fairman and Bert

Jaguar's most celebrated competition model, the 1954 XK120D (or D-type), photographed at the Motor Industry Research Association's Nuneaton test track.

ABOVE: *Stirling Moss sets out for a wet practice run at Dundrod, Northern Ireland, in the 1951 works XK120C (or C-type) competition model with which he was about to win the classic Tourist Trophy race. (He had won it the year before, in an XK120.)*

BELOW: *A Jaguar XK120 fixed-head coupé with alternative wire-spoke wheels (which require open rear wheel arches). This one had just averaged over 100 mph (160 km/h) for a whole week, driven by Stirling Moss and (seen here) Jack Fairman, Leslie Johnson and Bert Hadley (Paris, 1952.)*

ABOVE: *The Lyons sports cars: (from left to right) the XK120 of the early 1950s, the 1929 Austin Seven Swallow, and the 1971 Jaguar E-type V12 roadster.*

RIGHT: *Private entries used to be the rule rather than the exception in the Monte Carlo Rally. Here the Manchester butcher Charles Merrill and his friends arrive in France for the rally in 1955. A Mark Seven won this event in 1956.*

Hadley at Montlhéry, near Paris, in 1952, using one of the new XL120 fixed-head coupés.

Lyons's original idea of low-volume production for the XK120 did not work. Demand was too great. The alloy-over-timber bodywork was replaced by steel after 240 cars had been made; Jaguar would go on to make more than twelve thousand examples of the classic XK120.

From the XK120 Jaguar evolved two famous sports-racing cars, designed specifically to win the 24-hour race at Le Mans: the C-type (1951–3) and the D-type (1954–6). The C-type won the race in 1951 and 1953; then the D-type won it three times in succession, in 1955, 1956 and 1957. These cars had special lightweight body/chassis structures, but the engines were basically the production type. Their streamlined shapes were designed by Malcolm Sayer, an aerodynamics specialist.

While the prime purpose of winning Le Mans or any other competition was to publicise the product in a way that made it appear worthy throughout the world, there was another benefit. Technical development of components for safety and longevity on the road could be accelerated greatly through participation in endurance racing. In Jaguar's case, the best example of such a service to the everyday motorist was the race-proving of the disc brake principle, now virtually universal.

In 1954 the XK120, by then being offered with a choice of roadster, fixed-head or drophead coupé bodywork, began to benefit from its maker's experience and was replaced by the XK140, which had rack-and-pinion steering (instead of the less precise recirculating-ball type) and developed more power. Another version, the 1957 XK150, had disc brakes all round as standard.

The XK models remained in production until late 1960; over thirty thousand had been made by then. The series was now obsolescent. It was time for another sports-car revolution.

A table on page 37 shows the sequence of the XK series and its successors.

The Jaguar Mark Seven, as introduced in late 1950 at a list price of £1276, including tax. This is the car for which the XK engine was intended, although the XK120 roadster preceded it.

In 1955 William Lyons (soon to be knighted) and his Vice-Chairman (Engineering), William Heynes, compare their compact new Jaguar 2.4 saloon with a 1930 Austin Seven Swallow, at Browns Lane, Coventry.

EXPANSION

The XK engine with its brightly polished twin camshaft covers was not intended only for winning races and rallies, nor merely for a limited run of sports cars. William Lyons had been planning a completely new luxury saloon for many years, and the XK engine was an essential component. Its chassis was already well proved in the Mark Five which, for an interim model, had been a very fine car. The new saloon, which would ensure that Jaguar output reached a steady ten thousand cars a year by the mid 1950s, was announced towards the end of 1950 and named the Mark Seven, often written as Mk VII. (There was no Mark Six: Bentley was making one at the time.)

These were heady days for Jaguar, and there were many more to come, though there were some problems. The original Coventry plant off Holbrook Lane was outgrown by 1950, and all facilities were transferred during 1951-2 to a former Daimler factory 2 miles (3 km) away in Browns Lane; despite this inconvenience production continued to increase as scheduled. Lyons was lucky that his key production men, in particular John Sil-

ver, were of outstanding ability.

Another problem was the loss of production caused early in 1957 when fire destroyed one end of the main Jaguar car assembly hall. Yet shortened assembly lines were operating within two days, so that the 270 scrapped cars could be replaced quickly, and 1957 was another record year.

By that time the company had introduced the first compact Jaguar saloon since the old four-cylinder models had been phased out in early 1949. The so-called 2.4 saloon (actually nearer 2.5 litres) had a short-stroke version of the now universal XK engine, and it was the first Jaguar saloon to be built by the latest unit-construction methods. It had coil-spring independent front suspension and unusual cantilever leaf springs at the rear. Announced in September 1955, it was supplemented in 1957 by a powerful version featuring the familiar long-stroke 3.4 litre XK engine. The Jaguar 3.4 saloon was very fast and, as soon as they had been developed sufficiently, Dunlop disc brakes became a much needed option.

19

The two-tone Marks Eight and Nine looked identical, but the latter had a 3.8 engine and disc brakes. This example also has the special Harold Radford Countryman boot conversion.

Knighted in 1956, Sir William Lyons began to create the Jaguar Group of Companies in 1960 when he acquired the Daimler Company from its owners, the Birmingham Small Arms company. This made Jaguar the proprietor of Britain's longest-established motor company; Daimler provided a range of fine cars, buses and military vehicles and, above all, the space to expand yet again. Daimler's factory at Radford, Coventry, would house most of the group's manufacturing, while Browns Lane was turned over to assembly.

In 1961 and 1963 respectively Guy Motors of Wolverhampton and Coventry Climax Engines Limited were also bought. Guy, in liquidation, made reputable trucks, tractor units and buses (its next new range would be called Big J).

The Glasgow police force was one of many that used the compact high-performance Jaguar saloons of the late 1950s. On the right is the original (narrow grille, spatted wheel) 2.4, as introduced in autumn 1955. Next to it is a 1957 3.4, and beyond that, a pair of Mark Twos.

20

ABOVE: *The 3.4 and 3.8 litre Jaguar S-type saloons (1963-8) were, in effect, elongated Mark Twos with independent rear suspension.*

RIGHT: *A Jaguar 3.8 litre Mark Two on a record-breaking run at Monza in 1963, the year in which the German Peter Noecker became the first European touring car race champion, driving a similar vehicle.*

BELOW: *The final development of the compact theme: the 1966-9 Jaguar 420, with 4.2 litre XK engine and varying-ratio power-assisted steering.*

21

Coventry Climax had added to its fame in the field of fork trucks and fire-pump engines by producing some of the world's finest Grand Prix engines, as used by Cooper, Lotus and others. The engineering prowess of Coventry Climax was largely attributable to Walter Hassan, who had joined from Jaguar in 1950. It has been said half jokingly that one of Sir William's reasons for buying Coventry Climax was to get Hassan back on Jaguar's engineering team.

The Jaguar car range was rapidly modernised during the early 1960s. The sporting XK models and the large Mark Seven saloon (together with its successors the Marks Eight and Nine) had become outmoded by then and only the compact saloons, muddlingly re-launched as the Mark 2 in late 1959, were up-to-date when the new decade began.

At the Geneva Show in March 1961 Jaguar introduced the E-type, a new sporting roadster and coupé whose lithely curving lines attracted much press attention, just as the XK120 had done in 1948-9. The name suggested that this was another competition car but although it did win its first race, and despite looks reminiscent of the Le Mans-winning D-type, the E-type was essentially a grand touring car designed for two people to motor long distances in effortless comfort and security. It had the XK engine (in 3.8 litre triple-carburettor form) and disc brakes but there was a new all-

ABOVE: *A Jaguar Mark Ten and an E-type coupé in the Jura Mountains en route to a Geneva motor show.*
BELOW: *The Belfast salesman Brian McDowell with the first E-type to reach Northern Ireland, in 1961. The external bonnet lock gives away the car's age.*

22

Mark Twos and Mark Tens on the production line, about 1962.

independent suspension system which transformed the character of this and every subsequent new Jaguar. Later in 1961 the same suspension was applied to a new large saloon, the Mark Ten.

Jaguar had given up racing as a factory team in the late 1950s and had instead supported, to varying degrees, a number of private entrants, many of whom were very successful. The Mark 2 saloon was dominant in touring car marathons and was the choice of the first (1963) European Touring Car race champion, Peter Noecker, who shared the driving with Peter Lindner, Jaguar's German importer.

The E-type was not as adaptable to GT racing, however, and it was to a Le Mans sports prototype that Heynes turned. In 1964 his team designed a mid-engined prototype with a 500 brake horsepower double overhead-camshaft 5 litre V12 engine, but only one XJ13 was made. It was never raced, although it was tested in 1967 before becoming a museum piece. Having won Le Mans five times, Jaguar

was not keen to risk so soon the huge investment it would need to take on the might of Ferrari, Ford and Porsche, each of which had acquired large racing budgets since Jaguar's Le Mans days.

The compact range was expanded in 1963 with the launch of the S-type and in 1966 with the 420. Both were based on the Mark 2, but they had more passenger and luggage accommodation and they incorporated the new independent rear suspension which was proving so successful. The Mark Ten was restyled in 1966 and renamed the 420G. Naming its cars was never a Jaguar strong point.

In 1966 Sir Willam Lyons agreed with Sir George Harriman that his Jaguar group would merge with the British Motor Corporation, for long-term security with the promise of retained autonomy. Unfortunately BMC was about to make a huge loss, and Leyland Motors would soon become the dominant partner in the uneasy, government-encouraged alliance of 1968 — the formation of British Leyland Motor Corporation.

23

ABOVE: *The Jaguar XJ13, a mid 1960s competition prototype, photographed at the Motor Industry Research Association test track. It never raced, but it may have inspired competition cars twenty years later.*

OPPOSITE TOP: *This independent rear suspension assembly, with inboard disc brakes, was first used on the E-type and Mark Ten in 1961. All subsequent Jaguars (up to XJ40) have featured this system.*

OPPOSITE CENTRE: *The E-type owed much to the D-type competition model. More than a decade separates these two cars, that on the right being a 1967 4.2 litre model (headlamp covers deleted).*

OPPOSITE BOTTOM: *Jaguar 4.2 litre E-type 2+2, 1969 model.*

BELOW: *Jaguar's original four overhead-camshaft 5 litre V12 engine as fitted to the XJ13.*

25

Sir William Lyons, William Heynes and the engineering team with their 1968 masterpiece, the Jaguar XJ6.

THE XJ ERA

Jaguar was already planning the launch of its most important new model to date, the XJ6, when, in 1968, the company found itself in a new situation as part of British Leyland. Sir William Lyons was still in charge, however, and he directed a re-organisation of the model range, phasing out four saloons over a two-year period (the Mark 2, the S-type, the 420 and the 420G) and replacing them with one new one.

The XJ6 was given a favourable reception in September 1968. It was a fairly large saloon, though not as large as the 420G, and had the distinctive Jaguar look. Sir William had established a special indefinable set of traits for his marque, and the new car, with its crouching stance created by a haunch at the rear quarter, seemed to epitomise them. Another feature was the insulation of the occupant from road shocks, while retaining a complete sense of feel for the driver. (The master of Jaguar vehicle engineering was Robert Knight; he and Walter Hassan became heads of engineering on Heynes's retirement in 1969.)

At first there were 2.8 and 4.2 litre XJ6s, but the 2.8 litre XK engine was an unsatisfactory member of a family known for reliability, and in due course it disappeared, to be replaced by a 3.4 litre unit.

Jaguar's chief power unit engineer, Harry Mundy, had been working on a new V12 engine, and it was first used in the E-type in 1971. Turbine-smooth, the unit became the perfect partner for Knight's dynamic XJ saloon structure. In 1972 the XJ12 was introduced. It was voted Car of the Year.

Sir William Lyons retired in 1972. His deputy, Raymond England, replaced him, but on 1st October 1972 Jaguar Cars Limited ceased to exist as an individual company. England retired in 1974 and British Leyland was soon nationalised. Jaguar kept its independent spirit through those difficult times, and this was to stand it in good stead after (Sir) Michael Edwardes became head of British Leyland in late 1977.

Edwardes was the first British Leyland chief to recognise the need for individual-

26

ity in maintaining morale and enthusiasm. In 1980 he appointed John Egan to lead a new Jaguar company to successful independence or to close it down. There had been problems of production quality and low demand, due to a declining reputation, the oil embargo by the Organisation of Petroleum Exporting Countries (fortunately receding) and the problems of meeting the emission control and other legislative requirements in Jaguar's biggest export market, North America.

There was no longer a true sports car. The E-type had been replaced in 1975 by the XJ-S. This was a svelte coupé, adapted from the saloon range, but not nearly as attractive as the short-lived two-door XJ6 and XJ12 coupés, of which only just over ten thousand had been produced in the mid 1970s. Happily, the XJ-S was a marvellously roadworthy car and it became a great success.

In the early 1980s Egan approved a racing programme, with a view to a Jaguar driver becoming European Touring Car champion again. This was achieved, in an XJ-S, by the Scottish driver Tom Walkinshaw in 1984, the third season in which Jaguar had challenged their great market rivals, BMW, in what had become BMW's special domain.

In 1984 the Jaguar company was privatised. Properly financed, Robert Knight's successor and former protégé, James Randle, completed the engineering of the delayed XJ6 replacement with diligence; likewise Egan's deputy in charge of manufacture, Michael Beasley, transformed production facilities. Sir William Lyons saw his firm's recovery and approved the XJ40 (as the new model was coded in house) before he died in 1985.

At last, in 1986, the XJ40 was revealed and given a public name – XJ6. This was chosen on the basis of the success of the previous XJ6, which had been developed through Series Two and Three forms and was still selling in record quantities.

A new generation of six-cylinder engines (already in use in one form in the XJ-S) was introduced for the 1987 model saloon, together with many technological and safety features. The good looks, the comfort, the secure handling and braking and the excellent value for money showed that Jaguar had caught up with its competitors with its XJ40 range.

The British motor industry had suffered

For the sixtieth anniversary (1982) of his company's founding, Sir William Lyons was photographed with (Sir) John Egan, an early Jaguar 2.7 litre saloon and a modern Series Three XJ.

many problems, but record sales and profits made Jaguar an exception in 1985 and John Egan was knighted. In competition the Jaguar XJR V12 racing cars operated by Tom Walkinshaw Racing won the World Sportscar Championship in 1987 and 1988. 1988 was an outstanding year as Jaguars also won the 24-hour races at Daytona and Le Mans.

A cyclical weakening of the US dollar put sales and profits under pressure in 1988, however, and Jaguar's stock weakened. In the autumn of 1989 General Motors and Ford started bidding against each other to buy Jaguar, a situation that Sir John Egan and his board had to accept. Profits were small and could not support the huge investment programme that would be needed in the 1990s. Eventually a Ford takeover was negotiated, giving Jaguar a large degree of autonomy. The terms valued Jaguar plc at £1.6 billion and guaranteed the Coventry firm £1 billion over a period of years to produce the long-awaited new models.

The first of these did not appear until 1996, when the sleek, well-appointed XK8 was unveiled at the Geneva Motor Show. In the meantime the existing model line had been refined, and in 1993 work began on updating Jaguar's manufacturing facilities.

In 1990 the company had again won at Le Mans, with XJR-12s in first and second places, its seventh triumph in this event.

But recession returned to both sides of the Atlantic, and in 1992 just 20,601 cars,

15,981 Jaguars and 4620 Daimlers, left Browns Lane – an eleven-year low. Despite substantial losses, Ford held its nerve and, as the financial climate improved, in 1995 Jaguar moved back into the black and output rose to 41,023 cars.

The recession also affected sales of a 210 mph (338 km/h) XJ220 supercar. This had appeared as a 6.2 litre V12-powered mid-engined four-wheel-drive concept vehicle at the 1988 British motor show and predated the Ford take-over. However, the production coupé announced in 1991, to the disappointment of some, was less elaborate and had a 3.5 litre V6 engine and rear drive. The chilly economic climate prevented some prospective owners who had placed deposits from taking delivery. XJ220 manufacture ceased in 1994 after 275 examples had been built.

That year the mainstream XJ6 saloon was revised and endowed with new front and rear ends. There was a supplementary supercharged XJR version capable of over 150 mph (241 km/h). The V12-powered XJ12, enlarged to 6 litres for the XJ40 line in 1993, was perpetuated, but the engine was discontinued at the end of 1996 after a twenty-five year production life. This was because of the arrival, in March of that year, of a new Jaguar-designed 4 litre V8 engine, only the fourth power unit in the marque's history. This appeared in the XK8, which replaced the XJS (it lost its hyphen in 1991). Like its predecessor, the XK8 appeared in coupé and convertible forms, aimed at the high-performance sector. Further enhancement followed in

The Jaguar XJ6 in Series Three guise for the early 1980s, the period in which the company began to recover the ground it had lost under British Leyland.

28

The XK8, announced in 1996, produced in coupé and convertible forms and powered by a new Jaguar-designed 4 litre V8 engine. Top speed is 155 mph (241 km/h) and styling was the work of the company's Geoff Lawson.

1998 with the arrival of supercharged XKR versions.

The V8 was extended late in 1997 to the saloons, which were thus accorded the XJ8 prefix; this marked the end of a six-cylinder line that reached back to the marque's 1931 SS origins.

Jaguar's range was further expanded in spring 1999 with the arrival of the cheaper S-type saloon, which is built not at Allesley but in a new factory at Castle Bromwich, Birmingham, where the make's bodies are also produced. Corporate parentage is reflected by the fact that the S-type's plat-

form is shared with the in-house Lincoln LS luxury saloon. Power comes from the existing V8, with the alternative of a new American-built 3 litre V6 unit.

The high-specification XJ8, the Sovereign for 1999, at Jaguar's engineering centre at Whitley, Coventry, opened in 1988. The Sovereign model name had been previously applied in 1969 to the Daimler version of the Series 1 XJ6.

29

SWITCHBACK YEARS

Jaguar's recent past has arguably proved to be the most traumatic period in its history and drew into question Ford's overriding strategy for the company at a time when it was also grappling with its own managerial and financial problems.

Nick Scheele had been Jaguar's chairman since 1992 but in 1999 he was promoted to head Ford of Europe and Jaguar became part of the company's newly formed Premier Automotive Group (PAG). This embraced Aston Martin, purchased in 1987, the old-established Lincoln line and Volvo, which had joined the Ford stable in 1999. PAG's president was Wolfgang Reitzle, BMW's former head of research and development, and he accordingly became Jaguar's new chairman.

Because of the demand for the S-type, Jaguar production was increasing and doubled in the years between 1997 and 1999, when it rose from 43,551 cars built to 86,317. In addition quality was notably improved and, with a new executive smaller model, coded X400, in the offing, Jaguar looked likely to exceed the 100,000 car mark for the first time in its history. Even so, in 1993 the company had been predicting a figure of 200,000.

In June 1999 Jaguar's head of styling, Geoff Lawson, died suddenly from a stroke at the age of fifty-four. While he had given the marque a new and distinctive look, he was the first to recognise that his work had not always pleased Jaguar's traditional clientele. The lines of the XK8 had to some extent reflected Japanese and American themes although the S-type contained echoes of Jaguar's Mark 2 saloon of the 1960s.

Lawson was unrepentant. 'I've never been a fan of the British cars', he declared at the time of that model's launch; 'they didn't have an emotional tie for me. I've never owned one.' His forte was for American cars: he drove a Chevrolet Corvette to work. His place at Jaguar was taken by Ian Callum, who became director of design, not, he insisted, of styling. He had been responsible for the acclaimed lines of the in-house Aston Martin DB7 coupé and the impending Vanquish, to be launched in 2001.

Geoff Lawson therefore did not live to see his work reach fruition on the most important model of Ford's stewardship of Jaguar. Launched in February 2001, the X-type, built at Ford's plant at Halewood, Liverpool, should have transformed the company's prospects, pushing up volumes and giving Jaguar a range of three saloons to match the best that the German motor industry had to offer.

Alas, the X-type has not attracted the young executives in the numbers expected and American sales have not reached

Jaguar became a two saloon car company for the first time since the 1960s with the arrival in 1999 of the S-type. Sharing a platform with the in-house Lincoln, it is not quite as small as expected with a wheelbase 1.5 inches (40 mm) longer than the standard-bodied XJ8.

Inside the S-type with mirror-polished mushroom-stained bird's-eye-maple veneer dashboard and a particle-filtered automatic climate-control system.

anticipated targets. Potential customers have instead remained loyal to their BMW 3-series, Mercedes-Benz C-Class and Audi A4 saloons.

Knowing the formidable opposition it was to encounter, Jaguar daringly decided to launch the X-type with four-wheel drive as a standard fitment, a facility otherwise available within its market sector only on the more expensive versions of the Audi. Its provision drew the comment from *Autocar* magazine that the initiative would be judged by history to have been 'either inspired or foolhardy'. For while the actual and marketing advantage over the opposition was all-weather stability, this had to be balanced against extra cost, added weight and complication.

The X-type's platform was courtesy of Ford's successful second generation front-wheel-drive Mondeo family hatchback, even though initially this configuration was not considered to be appropriate for a sports saloon.

A sharing of such components is widely practised within the motor industry and makes sound economic sense, but the small Jaguar's partial Mondeo pedigree has remained a subject of ongoing criticism of the X-type and took some of the shine off the product.

However, its V6 engine was pure Jaguar, if US-built, and derived from the Whitley-designed V8 unit that had first appeared in the XK8. The six, available in 2.5 and 3 litre forms, was already being used in the S-type, although it was mounted transversely, instead of on a north/south axis. The X-type's rear wheels were driven through a viscous coupling via a split propeller shaft. In its most potent form it was a 145 mph (233 km/h) car.

If the model's mechanical specification was impressive, its appearance was more controversial. As will have been apparent, one of the key ingredients of Jaguar's appeal, ever since the launch in 1931 of the SS1, was the quality and individuality of its styling. And this new small car lacked the all-important element that had made the Mark 2 and original XJ6 saloons so distinctive. As a supremely talented stylist,

The X-type saloon was introduced in 2002 and was initially only available in four-wheel-drive form. This is the estate version, announced in 2004, and which, like the saloon, is offered with a choice of petrol and diesel engines.

Sir William Lyons had proved to be a very hard act to follow.

Visually the X-type is related to both the XJ8 and the S-type and, while it shares its quadruple headlights with the former, instead of being round they are ellipsoidal. As such, they are never wholly at ease with their immediate surroundings, and the contradictions apparent in its 'face', to quote stylistic parlance, unsettle the remainder of the four-door bodywork. Packaging, especially for back-seat passengers, and trim quality were also criticised by commentators.

For a year the four-wheel-drive X-type was the only version on sale but in February 2002 came a front-wheel-drive variant, needed to bolster the model's disappointing sales. The basic model, a 2 litre, sold for a shade under £20,000 and was therefore £2000 less than the cheapest four-wheel-drive model. The V6 engine endowed the car with a top speed in excess of 120 mph (203 km/h).

Then at the 2001 Frankfurt motor show Jaguar displayed its R-Coupe concept car, which pointed the way forward to a new stylistic direction for the company and effectively marked an end to the Lawson era. From then on Ian Callum's designs would be characterised by clean contours without so-called character lines and, while they looked to the future, the car's radiator grille was clearly inspired by the C-type sports racer of the 1950s. The aim was to attract well-heeled but elusive younger buyers to the marque.

Meanwhile there were other pressing problems to be addressed. Wolfgang Reitzle was also far from happy with the S-type, conceived prior to his appointment, and he considered that it required radical re-engineering to compete with the 5-series BMW produced by his former company. The first results were seen in spring 2001, the initial outcome being the S-type 3 litre V6 Sport, identifiable by a painted radiator grille, tweaked engine, ZF rather than Ford steering, and uprated interior. The last feature was extended to the mainstream model, which also benefited from the option of a ZF six-speed automatic transmission.

An even more potent version followed in the spring of 2002 in the form of the R model S-type with an enlarged 4.2 litre supercharged engine and suspension revisions. With a power unit developing 400 bhp, it made the R the most powerful ever Jaguar saloon, endowing it with a governed top speed of 155 mph (262 km/h) and a 0–60 mph (96 km/h) figure of 5.3 seconds.

This engine was extended during the year to the XK8 sports car, taking this XKR version into Ferrari and Porsche territory, the 4.2 litre engine also being available in unblown form.

Then in April 2002 came a corporate bombshell when Reitzle resigned the PAG presidency after a mere three years in the job. Amidst rumours of clashes with his boss, the former Jaguar chairman Sir Nick Scheele (knighted in 2001), who by then was corporate chief operating officer based in the United States, Reitzle was replaced by Mark Fields, who was credited with returning Ford's Mazda subsidiary to profit.

One of the casualties of Reitzle's departure was project X600, otherwise known as the F-type concept of 1999. Displayed at the 2000 Detroit motor show, this uncompromising small two-seater roadster was styled by Keith Helfet, who had collaborated with Geoff Lawson on the lines of Jaguar's XJ220 supercar. It was created with Porsche's mid-engined Boxster in its sights, and a launch date of 2004 was envisaged.

By the end of 2001 it had been reworked as a similarly mid-engined model but this low-volume car was finally abandoned in May 2002, following the departure of its sponsor. Resources would be thereafter channelled into offering diesel engine options for Jaguar's saloon car lines.

In 2003 the company built 126,121 cars, the highest in its history, but it had to absorb the overheads of three factories, namely Browns Lane, Castle Bromwich and Halewood. At this time Volvo, a fellow member of the Prestige Automotive Group, was producing some 400,000 vehicles from two manufacturing facilities.

The big news for 2003 was the new XJ saloon, announced at the 2002 Paris motor show. It closely resembled its predecessor and is therefore credited to the late Geoff Lawson, its lines being rooted in the original XJ6 of 1968. But the big technological difference was that its body was an aluminium monocoque, similar in concept to a steel structure. Instead of the individual components being welded together, the parts are bonded and riveted, a process that came from the aerospace industry. It therefore weighs just 485 pounds (220 kg), which was 308 pounds (140 kg) less than if it had been made conventionally. It accordingly weighed less than its smaller S-type stablemate and was structurally much stiffer.

While performance would benefit from such weight saving, above all this type of construction freed Jaguar from its reliance on Ford platforms, namely the Lincoln LS for the S-type and Mondeo for the X. In future the corporate tail would no longer wag the Jaguar and individuality could flourish. Although components would continue to be shared, they would be subordinate to the design rather than dominate it.

So much for the future. The XJ saloon's conservative appearance belied its advanced suspension. While there were double wishbones all around, instead of the usual coil springs air was the chosen medium to provide such refinements as self levelling and constant ride height facilities.

The new XJ's light weight meant that the 3 litre V6 from the S and X-types could be offered. Then there was a 3.5 litre V8 developed from its predecessor's 3.2, with a 4.2 above it and a top of range supercharged version, already used in the revised S-type and the XK8 sports car. ZF's latest six-speed automatic transmission came as standard, while top speed was 150 mph (241 km/h). A long wheelbase version followed for the 2005 season with the XJR's supercharged 4.2 litre under its bonnet.

Despite having embarked in 1993 on an £86 million five-year investment programme, Ford closed Browns Lane, Jaguar's car assembly plant since 1952, in 2005. Here these improved facilities aid the installation of the engine/gearbox unit in the XJ40 version of the XJ6 saloon.

Jaguar had long been criticised for not possessing a diesel option but in late 2003 the first fruits of Ford's joint programme with Peugeot-Citroen were unveiled. The X-type became the first saloon, in front-wheel-drive form, to be offered with such a facility, the engine being a 2 litre four-cylinder unit. Next, in May 2004, came an oil-burning S-type. In this instance power came from a twin turbocharged 2.7 litre V6. For 2006 this diesel was extended to the top of range XJ saloon.

An all-important X-type body variant arrived early in 2004 in the form of an estate car and to date the model has been the only saloon in the Jaguar range to be so enhanced.

However, 2004 was destined to be the nadir of Ford's stewardship of Jaguar. Against the background of PAG's soaring losses of £200 million in the second quarter of the year, of which some £138 million could be marked down to the Coventry company, in September the American multinational announced that it was to close the Browns Lane factory, Jaguar's home since 1952.

Ford also decided to sell Jaguar Racing, based at Milton Keynes, at the end of the year, after it had been beset by managerial and technological problems. It had been established in June 1999 and was the brainchild of Ford's then president, Jacques Nasser.The idea was to raise Jaguar's profile and to follow such mainstream manufacturers as Mercedes-Benz, BMW and Honda into Formula 1.

The racing stable established in 1997 by Jackie Stewart and his son Paul was purchased, but in its five-year life Jaguar Racing did nothing to enhance the prestige of the marque. Despite an outlay of £800 million, the V10 Cosworth-engined cars achieved only fourth and fifth placings aplenty but there was only one significant achievement: third place at the 2001 Monaco Grand Prix.

Jaguar car production at Browns Lane

Castle Bromwich, a former wartime Spitfire factory, is now the only Jaguar manufacturing plant in the Midlands. Here the bodyshell of the new XK is receiving attention.

ceased in the summer of 2005. Then in August the manufacture of the XJ saloon began at Castle Bromwich while the company's new sports car was being readied for production in a state-of-the-art facility.

But a year on, in August 2006, news broke that Ford's North American operations, having lost $2.2 billion (£1.3 billion) in the previous nine months, had appointed a former Wall Street banker, Kenneth Leet, to evaluate its corporate portfolio. It was feared that Jaguar might be put up for sale but in September Ford announced it was keeping the business. Instead it had decided to dispose of Aston Martin.

It was against such an unsettled background that in August 2005 Jaguar had unveiled its replacement for the XK8, a new sports car, which also bore the famous XK initials, the model going on sale early in 2006. The public had already had a preview at the 2005 Detroit motor show, when Jaguar displayed a concept XK coupé.

Lighter, faster and roomier than its predecessor, it featured, like the XJ saloon, an all-aluminium chassis with the body fastened by some 26,000 rivets, self-piercing screws and adhesive. It was also available in cabriolet (open) form. And

while the XK's magnificent lines were unquestionably twenty-first century, the distinctive oval nose harked back to the legendary sports racing Jaguars of the 1950s.

The 4.2 litre V8 engine, although reworked to give 295 bhp, was carried over from the XK8. This was mated to a six-speed ZF automatic gearbox with Formula 1 style paddle shift, making their first appearance on a Jaguar. The all-independent suspension was essentially taken from the XJ saloon. Top speed was limited to 155 mph (249 km/h) and the 0–60 mph (96 km/h) figure was claimed to be 5.9 seconds.

Above all the XK is the first production Jaguar to display the stylistic credentials of Ian Callum. A worthy recipient of the coveted Car of the Year accolade in 2006, and with commentators and potential customers alike praising its appearance, performance and refinement, the omens for its future look good.

But in October 2006 Alan Mulally, the former chief executive of Boeing who had been recruited to Ford to return it to profitability, cautioned that he would not provide further support for Jaguar, or for Land Rover, which Ford had acquired in 2000, unless they showed signs of improvement.

The architects of the new XK launched in 2006: Giles Taylor (left), Jaguar's senior design manager, and Ian Callum, design director, who had overseen Jaguar's recent stylistic transformation.

A new strategy is now in place with Jaguar taking as its example the financially buoyant Porsche company. The emphasis with future models will therefore be on lower volumes, combined, it is hoped, with much higher profitability, the new XK having set the stylistic pace. Jaguar built some 90,000 cars in 2005 and an output of about 70,000 per annum is now being contemplated. This is a far cry from the 200,000 units a year Ford envisaged back in 1993.

The new XK is available in open and closed forms. Their lines are unquestionably twenty-first century but display stylistic echoes from Jaguar's famous past.

JAGUAR SPORTS AND GT MODELS

model	body type	engine	announced	sold between model years
SS100	open two-seater	2.7 litre (1)	1935	1936 and 1940
SS100	open two-seater	3.5 litre (1)	1937	1938 and 1940
XK120	open two-seater	3.4 litre	1948	1949 and 1954
XK120	fixed-head coupé	3.4 litre	1951	1952 and 1954
XK120	drophead coupé	3.4 litre	1953	1953 and 1954
XK120C	racing two-seater	3.4 litre	1951	1952 and 1954
XK120D	racing two-seater	3.4 litre	1954	1955 and 1957
XK140	open/fixed-head/drophead	3.4 litre	1954	1955 and 1957
XKSS	racing two-seater	3.4 litre	1957	1957 (D-type conversion)
XK150	fixed-head/drophead	3.4 litre	1957	1957 and 1961
XK150	open two-seater	3.4 litre	1958	1958 and 1961
XK150S	open/fixed-head/drophead	3.4 litre	1958	1958 and 1961
XK150	open/fixed-head/drophead	3.8 litre	1959	1959 and 1961
XK150S	open/fixed-head/drophead	3.8 litre	1959	1959 and 1961
E-type	open/fixed-head	3.8 litre	1961	1961 and 1964
E-type	open/fixed-head	4.2 litre	1964	1965 and 1971
E-type	2+2 coupé	4.2 litre	1966	1966 and 1971
E-type	2+2 coupé	5.3 litre (2)	1971	1971 and 1973
E-type	open two-seater	5.3 litre (2)	1971	1971 and 1975
XJ-S	2+2 coupé	5.3/6 litre (2)	1975	1976 and 1996
XJ-S	2+2 coupé	3.6/4 litre (3)	1983	1984 and 1996
XJ-SC	cabriolet	5.3 litre (2)	1985	1985 and 1987
XJ-SC	cabriolet	3.6 litre (2)	1983	1984 and 1987
XJ-SC	convertible	5.3/6 litre (2)	1988	1988 and 1996
XJR-S	coupé	5.3/6 litre (2)	1988	1988 and 1994
XJ220	2 str coupé	3.5 litre (4)	1988	1991 and 1994
XK8	2+2 coupé	4.0 litre (5)	1996	1996 and 2002
XK8	convertible	4.0 litre (5)	1996	1996 and 2002
XKR	2+2 coupé	4.0 litre (6)	1998	1998 and 2002
XKR	convertible	4.0 litre (6)	1998	1998 and 2002
XK8	2+2 coupé	4.2 litre (5)	2002	2002 and 2005
XK8	convertible	4.2 litre (5)	2002	2002 and 2005
XKR	2+2 coupé	4.2 litre (6)	2002	2002 and 2005
XKR	convertible	4.2 litre (6)	2002	2002 and 2005
XK	2+2 coupé	4.2 litre (5)	2005	2006 on
XK	convertible	4.2 litre (5)	2005	2006 on

Most Jaguars had the XK double overhead-camshaft six-cylinder engine. Exceptions are indicated as follows: (1) overhead-valve six-cylinder engine; (2) V12 engine, enlarged 1993 and 1989 in Jaguar Sport XJR-S; (3) AJ6 six-cylinder engine, enlarged 1991; (4) turbocharged TWR V6 engine; (5) AJ-V8 engine; (6) supercharged AJ-V8.

To commemorate the fiftieth anniversary of the XK engine, Jaguar created the XK180 concept car, which drew the crowds at the 1998 British motor show. It was powered by the company's supercharged 4 litre V8 engine, and output was upped from 370 to 450 bhp. Its acclaimed lines are the work of Keith Helfet, who was responsible for styling Jaguar's sensational XJ220 supercar.

37

JAGUAR SALOONS AND CONVERTIBLE ADAPTIONS

model	body type	engine	announced	sold between model years
SSJaguar	saloon	1.6 litre (1)	1935	1936 and 1947
SSJaguar	saloon/tourer	2.7 litre	1935	1936 and 1937
SSJaguar	saloon/drophead	1.8, 2.7 and 3.5 litre	1937	1938 and 1940
Jaguar	saloon	1.8, 2.7 and 3.5 litre	1945	1945 and 1949
Jaguar	drophead	2.7 and 3.5 litre	1947	1948 and 1949
Mark Five	saloon/drophead	2.7 and 3.5 litre (2)	1948	1949 and 1951
Mark Seven	saloon	3.4 litre	1950	1951 and 1956
2.4	saloon	2.5 litre	1955	1956 and 1959
Mark Eight	saloon	3.4 litre	1956	1957 and 1958
3.4	saloon	3.4 litre	1957	1957 and 1959
Mark Nine	saloon	3.8 litre	1958	1959 and 1961
Mark 2	saloon	2.5, 3.4 and 3.8 litre	1959	1960 and 1967
Mark Ten	saloon	3.8 litre	1961	1962 and 1964
S-type	saloon	3.4 and 3.8 litre	1963	1964 and 1968
Mark Ten	saloon	4.2 litre	1964	1965 and 1966
420	saloon	4.2 litre	1966	1967 and 1968
420G	saloon	4.2 litre	1966	1967 and 1970
340	saloon	3.4 litre	1967	1968
240	saloon	2.5 litre	1967	1968 and 1969
XJ6	saloon	2.8, 3.4 and 4.2 litre (3)	1968	1969 and 1987
XJ12	saloon	5.3/6 litre (4)	1971	1972 and 1993
XJC	two-door coupé	4.2 & 5.3 litre (4)	1973	1975 and 1978
XJ6	saloon	2.9/3.6 litre (5)	1986	1987 and 1994
XJ6	saloon	4.0 litre (5)	1989	1989 and 1994
XJR	saloon	3.2/4 litre (5)	1988	1988 and 1992
XJ6	saloon	3.2 litre (5)	1990	1990 and 1994
XJ6	saloon	3.2 litre (6)	1994	1994 and 1997
XJ6	saloon	4.0 litre (6)	1994	1994 and 1997
XJR	saloon	4.0 litre (7)	1994	1994 and 1997
XJ12	saloon	6 litre (4)	1994	1994 and 1996
XJ8	saloon	3.2 litre (8)	1997	1998 and 2005
XJ8	saloon	4.0 litre (8)	1997	1998 and 2005
XJR	saloon	4.0 litre (9)	1997	1998 and 2005
S-type	saloon	2.5/3 litre (10)	1998	1999 on
S-type	saloon	2.7 litre D (11)	2004	2004·on
S-type	saloon	4.0 litre (8)	1998	1999 and 2002
S-type	saloon	4.2 litre (8)	2002	2002 on
S-type R	saloon	4.2 litre (9)	2002	2002 on
X-type	saloon	2 litre V6 (10)	2002	2002 on
X-type	saloon	2.5/3 litre 4 x 4 (10)	2001	2001 on
X-type	saloon	2/2.2 litre D (12)	2003	2004 on
X-type	estate	2/2.5 litre (10)	2004	2006 on
X-type	estate	2/2.2 litre D (12)	2004	2004 on
X-type	estate	2.5/3 litre 4 x 4 (10)	2004	2004 on
XJ	saloon	4.2 litre (8)	2002	2003 on
XJR	saloon	4.2 litre (9)	2002	2003 on
XJ	saloon	3.5 litre (8)	2002	2003 on
XJ	saloon	3 litre (10)	2002	2003 on
XJ	saloon	2.7 litre D (11)	2005	2006 on

Post-war Jaguars did not have the SS prefix. (1) Last side-valve engine. (2) Last push-rod engines. (3) 2.8 litre was dropped and replaced by 3.4 after an interval. (4) V12 engine, enlarged 1993. (5) AJ6 engine. (6) AJ16 engine. (7) Supercharged AJ16 engine. (8) AJ-V8, 3.5 litre version and enlarged to 4.2 litres, 2002. (9) Supercharged AJ-V8. (10) US-built V6. (11) Twin turbocharged V6 diesel (D) developed with Peugeot Citröen and (12) four cylinder version, enlarged 2005.

The mid-engined XJ220 supercar of 1991/4 undergoing high-speed testing. Power came from a turbocharged 3498 cc V6 developing 542 bhp. This Jaguar was not built in Coventry but at Bloxham, Oxfordshire, in a joint venture between the company and Tom Walkinshaw Racing.

FURTHER READING

Daniels, Jeff. *Jaguar: The Engineering Story.* Haynes, 2004.

Porter, Philip. *Jaguar E-type: the Definitive History.* Haynes, 1989 and 1995.

Porter, Philip. *Jaguar Sports Racing Cars, C-type, D-type, XK SS and Lightweight E-types.* Bay View Books/Porter and Porter, 1995 and 1998.

Porter, Philip. *XK8: The Authorised Biography.* Bay View Books, 1996 and 1998.

Porter, Philip, and Skilleter, Paul. *Sir William Lyons: The Official Biography.* Haynes, 2001.

Skilleter, Paul. *The XJ-Series Jaguars, A Collector's Guide.* Motor Racing Publications, 1984.

Skilleter, Paul. *Jaguar XJS, A Collector's Guide.* Motor Racing Publications, 1996.

Skilleter, Paul, and Whyte, Andrew. *Jaguar Saloon Cars.* Haynes, 1980 and 1987.

Thorley, Nigel. *Jaguar in Coventry: Building the Legend.* Breedon Books, 2002.

Whyte, Andrew. *Jaguar: The Definitive History of a Great British Car.* Patrick Stephens, 1980, 1985 and 1995.

Whyte, Andrew. *Jaguar Competition Cars* (two volumes). Haynes, 1982 and 1987.

Whyte, Andrew. *Jaguar SS90 and SS100 Super Profile.* Haynes, 1987.

Whyte, Andrew. *Jaguar XJ40: Evolution of the Species.* Patrick Stephens, 1987.

PLACES TO VISIT

Most motor museums of any size contain examples of significant Jaguar models, but those listed below are of particular interest. Intending visitors are advised to ascertain the opening times before making a special journey.

Cotswold Motor Museum, The Old Mill, Bourton-on-the-Water, Cheltenham, Gloucestershire GL54 2BY. Telephone: 01451 821255. Website: www.cotswold-motor-museum.co.uk

Coventry Transport Museum, Millennium Place, Hales Street, Coventry CV1 1PN. Telephone: 024 7623 4270. Website: www.transport-museum.com

Grampian Transport Museum, Alford, Aberdeenshire AB33 8AE. Telephone: 01975 562292. Website: www.gtm.org.uk

Jaguar Daimler Heritage Trust, Browns Lane, Allesley, Coventry CV5 9DR. Custodian of Jaguar's collection of historic cars. Viewing by appointment. Telephone: 024 7620 2141. Website: www.jdht.co.uk

Lakeland Motor Museum, Holker Hall, Cark-in-Cartmel, Grange-over-Sands, South Lakeland, Cumbria LA11 7PL. Telephone: 01539 558509. Website: www.lakeland-motormuseum.co.uk

National Motor Museum, Beaulieu, Brockenhurst, Hampshire SO42 7ZN. Telephone: 01590 612345. Website: www.beaulieu.co.uk

An S-type keeps company with its namesake, the original S-type of 1964/68, and a Mark 2 built between 1960 and 1967.